# A Sparrow Splashing

Shih Jingang

# A Sparrow Splashing

*A Sparrow Splashing*
ISBN 978 1 76041 496 2
Copyright © Shih Jingang 2018

First published 2018 by
**GINNINDERRA PRESS**
PO Box 3461 Port Adelaide 5015
www.ginninderrapress.com.au

# Contents

| | |
|---|---|
| Preface | 7 |
| Introduction | 9 |
| Little Pebble's Journey | 13 |
| The Seeker's Journey | 31 |
| The Teacher's Journey | 51 |
| Glossary | 66 |

# Preface

'Truth' is a word often thrown about in conversation as if it is something that can always be known with complete certainty. Now, what do you habitually use to ascertain the truth? Your senses, analytical thought, previous experience and the opinions of those you trust? But these things can often only give a superficial understanding of a subject or object.

The Buddhist nun Wu Jincang said to the Sixth Ch'an Honoured Ancestor Huineng, 'I have studied the Mahapari Nirvana Sutra for many years and yet I do not understand many parts of it. Please enlighten me.'

Honoured Ancestor Huineng responded, 'I am illiterate. Please read it out to me and perhaps I will be able to explain the meaning.'

The nun said, 'You cannot read, so how then will you be able to understand the meaning?'

Huineng replied, 'Truth has nothing to do with words. Truth is like the bright moon in the sky; and words are like a finger pointing to its location. However, the finger is not the moon. To look at the moon, it is necessary to gaze beyond the finger, right?'

The title of this book, *A Sparrow Splashing*, is like a finger pointing to the moon, as are the stories and teachings within. It looks at my life journey through the eyes of a child named Little Pebble; a young man called the Seeker; and the Teacher, a Buddhist Monk. The three of them have committed their lives to the path of a Bodhisattva, whose vow is to attain enlightenment for the benefit of all sentient beings. For Little Pebble, the Seeker and the Teacher, there is a finger pointing to some *thing*. What is it?

Shih Jingang

# Introduction

Walking along a garden path on a warm summer morning. Hear splashing water. See a sparrow joyfully flapping its wings in a birdbath. Sight and sound reverberates. All thoughts dissolve. All sight and sound is around and within. There is nothing that is not you, there is nothing that is you. There is only the sight and sound of a sparrow splashing in a birdbath filling the entire universe.

The above experience is natural with qualities of awareness, clarity and openness. It is also nameless: to try and grasp it with the thinking mind is to lose it. Attachment, anger and ignorance are what obscures the view into the ultimate nature of reality.

The Third Ch'an Honoured Ancestor Seng-T'san wrote, 'All is empty, clear, self-illuminating, with no exertion of the mind's power. Here thought, feeling, knowledge and imagination are of no value.'

To experience this, let go of dualistic thinking. Then there is no like or dislike, good or evil, subject or object, I or you. This is the mind before thinking, which sees things as they truly are. This is our True Self: the Buddha-mind. What is Buddha? A sparrow splashing in the birdbath.

An ageless karmic seed
Grows within a child,
Its branches made of dreams
Reaching to Become.

Its stem is called Desire,
Ignorance the root,
And now through eyes of wonder
The child will taste the fruit.

# Little Pebble's Journey

## The Teacup

One day Little Pebble and his Master, an old monk, were sitting together by a campfire, looking at the flames slowly rising and dissolving into space. Eventually, Little Pebble tired of the scene and turned to face his Master, who was sipping tea from a cup he was cradling with both hands.

A question formed in Little Pebble's mind. 'Master, where is Buddha?'

'In this teacup,' replied the old monk, indicating the cup he was holding.

Little Pebble climbed on to his Master's lap and pulled the cup down to his eye level. He peered inside the now empty vessel, not understanding, then looked up to meet the old monk's smiling eyes. Little Pebble again looked into the cup. It was still empty.

'The world is in this teacup,' his Master said. 'Keep looking.'

## The Tadpole Pool

Letting go is a difficult lesson. To achieve it is to clearly see things as they truly are, as they have come to be through causes and conditions.

One summer's day, Little Pebble and his Master went for a walk in the mountains through lush green alpine meadows where few people went. A carpet of wild flowers in bloom spread out before them, reaching up to drink in the warm rays of the sun. Little Pebble laughed with delight and ran ahead of the old monk, only slowing down to hop over the occasional small stream.

Eventually the meadow came to an end and the ground underfoot changed to a soft spongy moss-like growth, which surrounded a series of small clear pools.

Little Pebble stopped and listened to the sound of trickling water for a while. Some movement in one of the pools caught his eye and he moved closer to get a better look. Peering into the clear water, Little Pebble saw many tadpoles swimming near the surface and, in an instant, he reached down and tried to pick some up. Sediment at the bottom was stirred up and the clear water turned muddy. Little Pebble lost sight of the tadpoles in the murky water and he burst into tears, thinking he had killed them.

The Master caught up to his young disciple, who was crying and desperately trying to reach into the water in the hope of rescuing some of the tadpoles he could see near the surface. The old monk pulled Little Pebble away from the water.

'Master, please, they're dying!' cried Little Pebble, who tried in vain to reach out towards the water.

'Stop!' commanded the Master, and the boy ceased squirming and listened. 'Leave the water unstirred,' the old monk advised, 'and it will become clear.'

After a while, the water in the pool did indeed become clear again, as if it had always been so, and the tadpoles swam around unaffected.

Little Pebble learnt a valuable lesson, understanding that his Master was not just trying to teach him about tadpole pools. He was pointing to something much bigger. But the boy still did not quite understand, and the old monk knew.

'Little one,' he encouraged, 'keep looking.'

## Mud Dharma

One of Little Pebble's favourite activities was playing with mud. He loved the feel of it, the squelching sound it made when pressed between his fingers, and the different shapes he could mould from it.

On one particular occasion, when Little Pebble was shaping figures from mud, he saw his Master walking towards him and proudly held up two of his creations, 'This is Mummy. This is Daddy.'

The old monk looked at the figures and noticed another one on the ground nearby, 'And who is that?'

Little Pebble looked surprised, and said, 'You, Master, see,' as he held the figure up to him.

'Oh,' said the Master, 'and I see you.'

Little Pebble was confused because he had not made a figure representing himself. He looked around in the mud, but could not see himself.

'Yes,' said the Master, 'I see you, me, Mummy, Daddy. I see all beings.'

Little Pebble did not quite understand, so the old monk continued, 'See, you make shapes, give them names, but they are all made from the same substance. Earth, sky, sun, moon, you, me: all these things appear different but actually have the same essence. The whole universe is like this. Understand?'

Little Pebble did not quite understand and his Master could tell. 'Keep looking,' he encouraged.

## Happy Buddha

Happiness and sorrow are right where *You Are*. Just look through eyes of wonder at the Buddha within you.

Once the Master had told Little Pebble that Buddha is happy and this pleased him a great deal. But when the young disciple was taken to a temple for the first time, he was surprised to see the serious looks on the faces of the people there. Did they not know that Buddha is happy?

So when Little Pebble was introduced to the Abbot of the temple, he said, 'Buddha is happy. Why are people sad?'

The Abbot regarded the boy for a moment, and asked, 'Are you happy?'

'I feel sad with people,' Little Pebble replied.

'Then Buddha is sad with you,' said the Abbot, 'and when you are happy, Buddha is happy with you.'

Now Little Pebble smiled, because he knew why Buddha is happy, and said, 'Buddha wants to play now.'

## Death, No-death

One day, Little Pebble went to his teacher, and said, 'Master, my friend's dog Tiger died.'

The look on Little Pebble's face told the old monk that he was troubled. 'Little one, do you have any questions?'

'Master, where did Tiger go?'

'Where did you come from?' asked the old monk.

'From my mummy's tummy.'

'And where did Mummy come from?'

Little Pebble couldn't think of an answer.

The Master regarded his young disciple for a moment, then said, 'Remember when you made shapes with mud and named them Mummy, Daddy, Master?'

Little Pebble nodded.

'Remember,' said the Master, 'that you, me, Mummy, Daddy, and all sentient beings have the same essence, called Buddha-nature. Well, that does not die. But other things that are impermanent do die.'

'Why?' asked Little Pebble.

The old monk smiled, and said, 'See, all things born and created eventually die. Our bodies of skin and bone, the things we make, and even thoughts, are constantly changing and eventually die. The body of the dog named Tiger died and went back to the earth to help the trees, insects, animals and us live. So when you walk on the earth, eat a piece of fruit off a tree, see a beautiful flower, know that everything you see and touch is Tiger and all beings, even you. Understand?'

'Tiger is me,' said Little Pebble. 'Tiger is Master, Mummy and Daddy, all things. Tiger did not die.'

'You say Tiger did not die,' responded the Master. 'Can you pat this Tiger, or take him for a walk?'

'No,' reacted Little Pebble with a giggle.

The old monk regarded his young disciple for a moment, then said, 'If there is no dog, no name, no "thing" that you can see or touch, what is left?'

'The Buddha,' replied Little Pebble.

'I see your Buddha's body is long dead,' said the Master. 'What is left?'

But Little Pebble could not answer.

The old monk smiled, and said, 'The Buddha you have heard of was born, lived in a body like yours, and that body grew old and sick, eventually dying. But the Buddha-nature did not die. Why? Because it is unborn, uncreated, and cannot die. You, me, all sentient beings have Buddha-nature. So little one, there is death, and no-death. Do you understand?'

Little Pebble nodded.

'And where did Tiger go?' asked the Master.

'Woof, woof!' Little Pebble exclaimed, and they both laughed.

## True Compassion

One day, while out on a walk, Little Pebble and his Master came across the body of a dog on the road. It had clearly been run over by a car.

The old monk stopped to look at the body, put the palms of his hands together in prayer, and chanted, '*Om Mani Padme Hum, Om Mani Padme Hum, Om Mani Padme Hum…*'

Little Pebble knew that his Master's words were Buddha Avalokiteshvara's Mantra of Compassion, which he had been taught to chant daily for all sentient beings. He also remembered being taught about Avalokiteshvara's vow, which had been made before all the Buddhas of the ten directions: 'May I help all beings, and if ever I tire of this great work, may my body be shattered into a thousand pieces.'

This story was one of Little Pebble's favourites, because it is said that Avalokiteshvara saved countless suffering beings. But when Avalokiteshvara saw that there were many more, he felt so upset that, for a moment, he almost lost faith in his vow, and his body did explode into a thousand pieces. In desperation, he called out to all the Buddhas for help. They came from all the directions of the universe to save him. With their great power, the Buddhas put him back together again, but this time he had eleven heads and a thousand arms, and on the palm of each hand was an eye that could see all suffering beings.

In this form, Avalokiteshvara felt more empowered than before to help all beings and, with great compassion, he vowed before all the Buddhas, 'May I not attain final Buddhahood until all sentient beings have attained enlightenment.' His intense feelings of great sadness for the pain of suffering beings caused two tears to fall from his eyes. Through the blessings of the Buddhas, these were transformed into Green Tara and White Tara: emanations of perfect compassion in feminine form.

'*Om Mani Padme Hum, Om Mani Padme Hum, Om Mani Padme Hum...*'

Little Pebble heard the compassion in his Master's voice and, as he looked down at the body of the dog, he felt very sad, put the palms of his hands together in prayer and joined in. '*Om Mani Padme Hum, Om Mani Padme Hum, Om Mani Padme Hum...*' Tears started rolling down Little Pebble's face.

The Master noticed and stopped the chant. Then he bent down and wiped the tears away from the cheeks of his young disciple. 'Little one,' said the old monk, 'are you all right?'

'I'm very sad, Master.'

'Why are you sad, little one?'

The young boy was surprised by the question, and said, 'I feel sad for the dog.'

'Is the dog still suffering?' asked the old monk.

'No, but the dog...' said Little Pebble, before his Master interrupted.

'Dog-nature is dead. That is past. Buddha-nature is alive. We pray that this sentient being and all beings attain a good rebirth. Little one, do you understand?'

This time, his young disciple understood. The old monk reached out and lovingly embraced Little Pebble.

## The Picture On the Wall

One day, while Little Pebble and his Master were out taking a walk, as they passed by an old house, a woman met them at the entrance. She bowed with the palms of her hands together in prayer, and said, '*Namo Amida Butsu, Namo Amida Butsu.*'

Neither Little Pebble nor his Master had ever heard these words before, but they were said with a beautiful smile and with such a genuine and loving heart that, when the woman invited them into her house, they were happy to accept.

The woman escorted her guests into the living room and they sat down while she went to the kitchen to get some tea and cake for them. While she was gone, Little Pebble casually looked around the room, until his eyes fixed themselves on a picture hanging on one of the walls. He walked over to get a better view and was awestruck by what he saw.

By now, the woman had returned to the living room with a tray of tea and cake, but Little Pebble had not noticed, so fixated was he by the picture.

The Master called out to his young disciple, 'Little one, have some cake.'

But the boy was far away, on a narrow white bridge surrounded by a raging river of fire to his left and torrents of water to his right. Looking behind, he saw bandits and wild animals waiting for him back on the eastern shore where he had come from. With nowhere left to run, he froze in fear...

'Little Pebble!' the Master called out more loudly, but still his young disciple did not hear him.

Then a woman's voice gently embraced Little Pebble and he found himself looking into the eyes of Great Compassion. '*Namo Amida Butsu, Namo Amida Butsu...*'

All feelings of fear dissolved into space, as if they had never really existed, and he saw himself crossing safely to the other shore.

## Karma For Sale

One day, Little Pebble told his Master about something he had heard a group of adults discussing at a temple. 'I heard some people say they were buying good Karma. How much is it?'

The old monk burst out laughing and nearly fell off his meditation cushion. It took him some time to recover, but when he did he said, 'Little one, tell me, who creates your Karma in the past, present, and future?'

'I do,' replied his young disciple.

'Good, and how much gold do you have?' asked the Master.

'None,' answered Little Pebble with a concerned look on his face.

'That's OK,' said the old monk with a reassuring smile. 'I have no gold, but it doesn't matter. See, Karma can't be bought or sold. We are responsible for our own Karma.'

'But people at the temple…' started Little Pebble, before his Master interrupted.

'That view is wrong. See, if I give something to others thinking I will be rewarded, or think I can buy Nirvana, then the motivation is not pure. That will not create good Karma. Only with selfless intentions can actions of body, speech and mind purify bad Karma, creating good. In practice, dedicate any merit to all suffering beings. Little one, why do that?'

'Because,' replied Little Pebble, 'all beings are my sister, brother, mother, father from a previous life.'

'Good, good,' said the Master, 'more precious than gold.'

## If-only-mind

One day, Little Pebble overheard groups of men and women talking as he wandered around the grounds of a temple.

'If only I had been born a man,' said one woman, 'then I could have become a monk and had a chance to attain enlightenment. Oh well, maybe in the next life.'

'And if only I didn't have children,' complained another woman, 'then I would be able to practise meditation.'

Little Pebble went over to a group of men who were busy talking.

'If only I hadn't got that girl pregnant as a teenager,' said one of the men, 'then I would have become a monk, and been happy.'

'And if only I didn't have so many bills to pay,' moaned another man, 'then I would be able to take time off work to go on retreat.'

After listening to the complaints of the men and women, Little Pebble went looking for his teacher and, by the time he found him, he was bursting to ask a question. 'Master, why are people unhappy?'

'Little one,' said the old monk, 'who is unhappy?'

'People here,' replied his young disciple.

'How do you know that?' asked the old monk.

'I heard them talking,' replied the boy, who then repeated in detail what he had heard.

Then the Master said, 'Little one, everything is practice. All through this life, there are countless opportunities to practise the Dharma. But when people live in if-only-mind, they create much suffering for themselves and others. If-only-mind is what Buddha called Dukkha, which are dissatisfied thoughts that say, "If only I was, or was not, a man, woman, father, mother, monk, rich, poor..." Many beings are never satisfied with what they have, and desire what they do not have. All sentient beings have Buddha-nature, but have different Karma, so need to work with what they have got. There is much to learn. Practise, practise... Understand?'

'Yes, Master. Thank you,' said Little Pebble, respectfully bowing to his teacher.

## The Constipated Meditator

Little Pebble could sit still longer than anyone, even longer than his Master. He had carefully studied the meditation posture of Buddha images and could copy them perfectly. So, in the mind of Little Pebble, he was like a Buddha.

But the Master could see the true face of his disciple so that, on one occasion when he saw him appear to be sitting in meditation, he said, 'Little one, are you constipated?'

'No, Master, I am like Buddha,' came the reply, his young face contorted in pain and irritation.

The old monk picked up a mirror and held it before Little Pebble's face, so that he saw reflected his foolish pride.

'Now closer to Buddha. Keep looking,' the Master encouraged.

## Compost Buddha

For Little Pebble, lessons on pride took a while to have an effect on him. But one day the Master found a way to get through to his young disciple, when the boy announced from his throne-like cushion, 'I am Buddha.'

'Who is?' asked the old monk.

'I am,' replied Little Pebble, expecting to be congratulated for his great achievement.

But instead, his Master demanded to know, 'Where is this "I" you speak of?'

'Sitting here, like Buddha,' answered Little Pebble.

'Oh!' said the Master, 'only like Buddha. So you are Not-Buddha.'

'Sitting still, I am Buddha!' asserted Little Pebble.

'Come with me, Sitting Buddha,' said the old monk, and Little Pebble followed his teacher outside into the garden.

'Here is your throne,' declared the Master, indicating a compost heap. 'Buddha, please sit.'

'But Master, I...' Little Pebble tried to protest.

'A Buddha can go anywhere, sit anywhere,' stated the old monk.

So Little Pebble sat down on the compost heap. It was not long before a lizard appeared, instinctively crawling up one of his legs.

'Buddha, how do you feel?' asked the Master.

'It's moving,' complained Little Pebble, with a concerned look on his face.

'What is moving?' asked the Master.

'A lizard is...' Little Pebble began, before being interrupted.

'No, little one, it is your mind that is moving. Understand?'

His young disciple blushed, realising his foolishness.

## The Sutra Reader

One day, Little Pebble observed his Master reciting the Heart Sutra. It sounded beautiful, and the young disciple was especially impressed with the fast speed with which the old monk recited the text.

Little Pebble decided to learn how to chant just like his Master, and started to practise on his own, concentrating on pronunciation of the words in the text and on speed. Every day, he would practise. Before long, he began to notice some improvement.

Several weeks later, Little Pebble had taught himself to recite the Heart Sutra very fast. He was filled with pride and excitement at his achievement. Now he wanted to share the good news with his teacher and when he found him, he called out, 'Master, I know the Heart Sutra!'

'Good, good,' said the old monk. 'Now show me its essence.'

Little Pebble could not think of anything to say.

'Little one,' the Master began, 'form is emptiness, emptiness is form. What are you attached to?'

Again the young disciple could not think of an answer. He was not even aware that he was attached to anything. The Master had quoted directly from the Heart Sutra, trying to encourage Little Pebble to study the text and look beneath surface appearances.

'Little one, you are attached to form, and have forgotten to look for the meaning of the Sutra. To be attached to form, or emptiness, creates more suffering for yourself. Buddha taught about suffering and the way out of suffering. The words only point to something. Look beyond. Understand?' The Master looked into the eyes of his young disciple and saw that he did not quite understand. 'Keep looking, little one. Practise, practise.'

## What is a Real Monk?

When Little Pebble was about eight years old, he overheard some monks at a temple talking about who they considered to be a real monk. They said that some monks from other traditions were not real monks.

Poor Little Pebble did not know what to think. Confused, he went looking for his Master and when he found him, he said, 'Master, what is a real monk?'

'Little one, why this question?' asked the Master.

'I heard monks at a temple say what a real monk is,' replied Little Pebble.

'Oh,' his Master said, 'that is a wrong view. If I think I am better, and my school or lineage is the best, then in ignorance I am the least. What matters are one's intentions to practise the Dharma and attain Buddhahood for the benefit of all suffering beings. Understand?'

'But Master, what is a real monk?'

'Little Pebble, this is attachment to appearances. Look beyond it.' The Master stared into the eyes of his young disciple, and asked, 'What is a monk?' And before Little Pebble could reply, his Master said, 'No-monk.'

## Truly Seeing

One day, while Little Pebble and his Master were walking through a garden, the old teacher stopped to look at a white rose in full bloom. He motioned for his young disciple to join him, and they both sat down near where the flower was growing.

'Little Pebble,' said the Master, 'when you look at this object, tell me what you think about it.'

'The flower is pretty,' stated the boy. 'I like it.'

'"Flower," you say. "Pretty, like it," you say,' replied the Master, looking to see how his young disciple reacted. Then he added, 'Mind creates names like flower, and thoughts of like and dislike, pretty and ugly. This mind is small and closed, but if you can see beyond it to the nature of mind, then all is vast like space, completely open to all things. In this state of awareness, there is neither a flower nor a non-flower. Understand?'

But the young disciple did not quite understand, so his Master continued, 'Little one, come here each day, and observe this flower. It will be your teacher. Watch it closely, then show me what its teaching is. OK?'

Little Pebble did exactly as he was told and returned each day to closely observe the flower in the garden. As time passed by, the white petals of the rose slowly began to change colour and shape as it decayed and eventually died.

During this process, something was also changing within Little Pebble as he witnessed the natural cycle of decay and death, which helped him to appreciate the short-lived fragility of the flower. At first he perceived the flower as beautiful, and its death as ugly. Then he saw the fragility of the flower as ugly, and great beauty in its death. Finally he realised that every stage in the life cycle of the flower was neither beautiful nor ugly. This awareness extended to seeing the flower, himself, and all other beings in a constant state of change: birth, the fullness of life, decay, death and rebirth. He saw the natural world around and within himself, as if for the first time, interconnected and interdependent in countless ways.

When the young disciple eventually returned to his Master, the old monk could tell that something had changed in him. 'Oh!' exclaimed the Master, 'I see that the flower is a great teacher,' and he bowed respectfully in the direction of the garden.

Little Pebble followed his example.

## Sending and Taking

One day, Little Pebble heard from his Master that there are old people in this world who live alone with no one to visit them. The news made his young disciple feel a compassionate urge to visit elderly people and dedicate his practice to them. When he told the Master of his intentions, he received his blessing.

'Go, little one, in the knowledge that all the Buddhas of the ten directions are with you. May your Bodhisattva practice bear fruit. May you take on the suffering of other beings and send all of your happiness to them.'

Little Pebble understood what his Master had said and took it as advice on how best to practise. So when he started visiting a sickly old woman who lived nearby, the young boy dedicated all of his efforts to trying to alleviate her suffering.

She appreciated Little Pebble spending time with her each day and would often affectionately hold his hand. While she did this, he would secretly visualise taking upon himself all her pain and suffering in the form of hot black toxic smoke. He would breathe this in and imagine it settling near his heart. Then this hot black toxic smoke would merge with his own negative Karma and be transformed into a cool pure healing light, which he would send to her as he breathed out.

The ancient practice of Sending and Taking had great meaning for Little Pebble and, although still a child, he could feel its profound potential to heal with pure compassion those who it touched. But however powerful this practice was, it could not protect the woman from sickness and old age and the boy realised that her condition was slowly deteriorating. One day, while the old woman held his hand, her eyes met his and a beautiful smile came to her face. In that moment, she died peacefully. Little Pebble was not sad. He knew it was the old woman's time and her Karma from this life had ripened and borne fruit, just as it would one day for him.

The boy remembered a profound teaching from his Master that gave his practice meaning: 'All sentient beings are your sister, brother, mother, father from a previous life. Give all your happiness to them and take all their suffering upon yourself, as a mother would for her only child.'

## Clouds and Rainbows

One day, when he was about ten years old, Little Pebble joined the Master to practise in his windowless retreat cell. But the young disciple could sense that something was different about his teacher. He seemed frail and sick.

Then the old monk said, 'Little one, the Karma of this life has ripened for me and I can feel that it is time to leave this body.' The Master could see the shocked expression on the face of Little Pebble, but continued with his teaching. 'Don't be sad, little one. You know that it is in the nature of all created things to decay and die, and this body is no different. Do you understand?'

Little Pebble nodded.

Then the Master said, 'You know, little one, that I will always be with you in your mind and heart.'

The boy felt encouraged.

'Now I need you to listen carefully,' advised the Master. 'For the next three days, I will merge the nature of my mind with the space of truth. I want you to lock the door of this cell and not open it until after sunset at the end of the third day. There will be no body left, so no funeral will be necessary. Understand?'

The young disciple nodded.

'Little one,' said the Master, 'on each of the three days I want you to gaze at the sky. On the first day, Buddha-like compassion will appear as a diamond sceptre cloud. On the second day, Buddha-like wisdom will appear as a cloud in the shape of a hand bell. And on the third day, the Buddha, Dharma and Sangha will appear as three interlinked rainbows over this cell.' The Master's final words were, 'Little one, in the Buddha, Dharma, and Sangha, the path and the purpose are one. Practise diligently.'

Wiping tears from his eyes, Little Pebble got up and locked the door of his Master's retreat cell from the outside.

Over the next three days, the young disciple gazed at the sky as instructed, and it happened exactly as his Master had said. It left Little

Pebble feeling a sense of wonder and inspiration, which lessened the pain of losing his beloved teacher. Then on the third day, as the sun disappeared over the horizon, the young disciple unlocked the door of his Master's retreat cell and looked inside. There was no one, nothing but a sweet scent left in the air, unlike anything the boy had ever smelt before.

For Little Pebble, although deeply feeling something treasured had been lost, part of him also knew that something even more precious had been gained. He felt immense gratitude to his Master and determined to continue building upon the firm foundation of practice he had been given, wherever the journey might lead.

Running towards…
Running away…
A desire for Attainment
Lived in a dream.

A forest of Pride,
A forest of Ignorance,
Carried by the Seeker
And yet Home is near.

# The Seeker's Journey

## The Fearful Old Monk

The Seeker left his home to go on retreat in the forest and on the way he met an old monk living alone in a large golden temple. He put the palms of his hands together and bowed respectfully to him. 'Good morning, noble sir,' said the Seeker as he approached.

'Why are you here?' challenged the old monk.

'Just passing through,' replied the Seeker.

'On what business?' asked the monk.

'I am going on a forest retreat,' said the Seeker.

'Don't go into the forest!' warned the monk. 'Stay here with me in the temple.'

'The Buddha once lived in a forest,' said the Seeker.

'But it is dangerous!' exclaimed the old monk.

'So, you have been there?' asked the Seeker.

'No,' replied the old monk.

'But your mind is there now,' said the Seeker, before bowing, and continued on his way.

## The Guest Monk

The Buddha's teaching on Dukkha, the dissatisfied mind, is profound in its scope. Sentient beings experience Dukkha in countless ways – as children, adults, monks, lay people – but are often unaware of it, and so miss opportunities to learn important lessons on the journey through this life.

One day while walking through the forest, the Seeker came

upon a clearing where a monastic community was living behind a large protective stone wall. He had heard of these monks, who had a reputation for being strict about keeping their rules of conduct, and were said to be living as the Buddha had done 2,500 years before. The Seeker was delighted to have the chance to meet and learn from them.

As the Seeker approached the entrance gate to the monastery, he was met by a young monk who seemed slightly irritated by his presence.

But he summoned up part of a smile to greet the visitor. 'Welcome. I am the Guest Monk.'

The Seeker put the palms of his hands together and bowed respectfully. 'Good morning, sir,' said the Seeker. 'Can I stay here with your community a while, to study and practise?'

'Certainly,' said the Guest Monk, 'as long as you are able to live as we do.'

'I will do my best,' said the Seeker.

'Good,' said the Guest Monk. 'Now follow me and I will take you to the sleeping quarters for visitors.'

The Seeker followed the young monk through the entrance gate and they walked down a series of steps cut into the hillside, passing a temple, into a cleared area of the forest where some retreat cabins had been built.

The Guest Monk stopped outside one of the cabins, and said, 'This is where you will sleep.'

'Thank you, sir,' said the Seeker.

'Do you have any questions,' asked the Guest Monk, 'before I get back to some real practice?'

'Yes, sir, I do,' replied the Seeker. 'What is "real practice"?'

'Why, meditation of course!' exclaimed the young monk, surprised by the question.

'Oh,' said the Seeker, 'then is helping visitors not real practice?'

Irritated by the question, the young monk said, 'Look, meditation is the way to enlightenment. Fortunately, I only have to do Guest Monk duties for a year.'

The Seeker bowed respectfully, and said, 'Sir, thank you for your teaching,' before he went inside the guest cabin, leaving the dissatisfied Guest Monk to wander away.

## The Abbot's Shrine

Attachment can take many forms and all sentient beings are capable of falling victim to its allure.

One day an old monk came to the Seeker's cabin, and said, 'I would like to show you a special place, where our Abbot once lived.'

'Thank you, sir,' said the Seeker, who bowed respectfully to him.

The old monk took him through the forest and, when they eventually arrived at a small clearing, the old monk stopped and proudly said, 'Ah, good. We're here.'

The Seeker was surprised to see nothing but some rusty old sheets of iron. 'Would you like me to clean up this mess?' asked the Seeker.

'No, of course not!' exclaimed the old monk. 'The Abbot wants this left here. It was his home.'

'Oh, I'm sorry.'

'Never mind.'

Not long after, the Seeker said, 'Sir, is the Abbot a very short man?'

'No, he is of average height,' replied the old monk, a little confused.

The Seeker paused for a moment, then said, 'Hmm, the Abbot must be strong to carry all of this around for many years.'

By now the poor old monk had no idea what the Seeker was talking about and took what he had said to mean carrying the monastic community. 'Yes,' agreed the old monk, 'the Abbot is a strong man and we are fortunate to receive his teachings.' Then he bent down and gently touched the rusty old sheets of iron.

'Thank you for showing me your Abbot's home,' said the Seeker.

## Sweeping Practice

One day, while the Seeker was out walking around the monastery, he noticed that quite a few leaves were scattered on a path the monks often used and decided to do some sweeping practice. He went to a shed where he knew various tools were stored and returned with a broom.

In a nearby cabin lived a young Postulant, who noticed the Seeker sweeping leaves from the path. 'You don't have to do that!' he called out.

But the Seeker did not respond, as he was trying to focus his attention on the act of sweeping and saying the ancient mantra of boundless light to himself, '*A-mi-ta-bha, A-mi-ta-bha...*' in time with each brushstroke.

The Postulant noticed the Seeker's lips moving but could not hear what he was saying. Curious, he came out of his cabin to take a closer look and, still not understanding, blocked the path of the Seeker. 'What are you doing?' the young Postulant demanded.

'Talking to you,' replied the Seeker.

'What are you holding on to?' asked the Postulant, indicating the broom.

'Nothing,' replied the Seeker.

'No,' said the now frustrated Postulant, 'what were you doing?'

'Oh, just sweeping some dust from my eyes,' replied the Seeker, before bowing to the young Postulant. Then he returned to his practice. '*A-mi-ta-bha, A-mi-ta-bha...*'

## The Gardener

Every morning, a small community of women who lived outside the monastery walls would bring food in because the monks were not allowed to prepare and cook meals for themselves or others.

The Seeker would observe these women walk through the entrance gate and wondered where the food offerings they brought with them came from. Did the women grow their own fruit and vegetables?

One day, the Seeker waited for the line of women to pass by and noticed an elder of the community walking slowly behind. He approached her, bowed, and said, 'Honoured Mother, thank you for the work you do for the monastery.'

'It is nothing,' she humbly replied.

'But without you and your sisters,' said the Seeker, 'the monks would starve.'

The old woman laughed, and said, 'The source of our good fortune comes from the work of the Gardener.'

'The Gardener, is he a monk?' asked the Seeker.

'You should find out for yourself,' advised the old woman, who pointed in the direction she wanted him to go.

After the midday meal, the last of the day, the Seeker walked in the direction the old woman had earlier suggested and found himself in a part of the monastery he had not been to before. A small path led him through some woodland and, on the other side, in a large clearing, was a beautiful garden where fruit trees and vegetables were growing in neat rows.

It was very quiet and at first there seemed to be no one around. The Seeker stopped walking and listened carefully. He could hear a slight sound of rustling in the branches of a tree and, on investigation, he found an old man picking fruit and putting it in a sack. The Seeker bowed respectfully, and said, 'Honoured Father, good day. Are you the Gardener?'

The old man returned the bow and laughed playfully like a little boy but said nothing. He then handed the sack to the Seeker and calmly went back to picking fruit from the tree. At first the young man didn't know what to think of the behaviour of this elder and found himself lost in thought, trying to think of something to say to get a conversation started. If this was the Gardener, then the Seeker wanted to ask him about his life. Maybe, he thought, there would be a chance to speak if he joined the old man in work.

However, as the Seeker helped the old man with his picking, thoughts and questions naturally dissolved into space. In their place was a deep awareness of the graceful movement of his own arm and hand removing fruit from the tree and placing it into the sack. Back and forth his body moved, like a graceful bird in flight. Eventually, even the rustling sound of the tree branches disappeared until there was only the movement of the young man's body picking fruit from a tree filling the entire universe.

The Seeker followed the old man around the garden, but not a word was spoken and it did not matter. Something profound was being transmitted to the young man from the uncontrived heart of the Dharma.

Later, when it was time to leave the garden, the Seeker bowed again to the old man and once more it was returned with the gift of a child's playful laughter.

## Dana Games

The Seeker found out that it was forbidden for men to visit the community of women, who lived outside the walls of the monastery. So the only contact he was able to have with them was when they came through the entrance gate each day to offer food to the monks. This formed an important part of the women's practice, called Dana: the act of generous giving.

But sometimes the importance of the motivation behind the act of giving is overlooked, or forgotten. It should be done selflessly, without any expectation of a reward. In this case, the reward being good Karma, which can only be earned if the intention is pure.

One day, the Seeker watched on as the women came as usual with their food offerings. They entered a hall and put their plates of food on large tables before going back outside, where the monks were waiting in line, and placed cooked rice in their alms bowls. The monks entered the hall and helped themselves to the food, while the women waited patiently outside. Once the monks departed, the women went back into the hall to eat what was left.

At the start of this ritual, the Seeker noticed one of the women moving her sisters' plates further down the table when they were not looking, so that her food offering was the first one the monks came across. No matter what, this woman seemed determined to be first in line. Did she believe that this would earn herself the reward of good Karma at the expense of her sisters? The Seeker had also observed her sampling food from the plates of the other women behind their backs. In so doing, she ate before everyone else, including the monks! Eventually, when the women left the hall, she had a look of great satisfaction on her face.

The Buddha had something to say about giving and sharing:

> O monks, if people knew, as I know, the results of giving and sharing, they would not eat without having given, nor would they allow the stain of stinginess to obsess them and take root in their minds. Even if it were their last morsel, their last mouthful, they would not eat without having shared it, if there were someone to share it with. But, monks, people do not know, as I know, the result of giving and sharing; they eat without having given, and the stain of stinginess obsesses them and takes root in their minds. (Itivuttaka Sutta 26:18–19)

## The Monk's Axe

Attachment to things, ignorance of the way things truly are, and anger, cause much suffering to sentient beings in Samsara. Indeed, a master once said of anger, 'Think of the habit energy of anger as a cannibal, who eats beings from the inside out.'

In the monastery lived a small group of old laymen who acted as caretakers doing work that the monks were not allowed to, such as turning the soil.

One day, two of the caretakers were asked to remove tree stumps from an area of the forest within the grounds of the monastery. Using an axe that had been donated to the monastery, the laymen set about their work with enthusiasm. But it was not long before the sound of a man's screaming voice could be heard through the forest.

The Seeker was not far away and rushed to help whoever was in distress. As he got closer, it sounded like someone was in great pain.

But on arrival, to his surprise, he found one of the monks holding an axe, shouting and gesticulating wildly at the two old laymen, 'You've ruined it, you've ruined it!' he screamed, veins bulging from his neck. Then the monk turned to face the Seeker, and said, 'Look what they've done to my new axe!' pointing to the blade, which had been slightly damaged.

'Whose axe?' asked the Seeker.

'Didn't you hear me? They've broken my axe!' exclaimed the monk, not understanding.

The Seeker paused for a moment, regarding the monk, then calmly said, 'Are you hurt?'

'What?' said the monk in disbelief.

'I heard you screaming in pain,' said the Seeker. 'Should I get a first aid kit?'

'Grrr!' the monk exclaimed in frustration and embarrassment, and stormed off into the forest alone.

The two old laymen looked at the Seeker with gratitude and relief, and one of them said, 'Thank you. For a moment, I thought we were going to die.'

'No,' replied the Seeker, 'it is not you who is dying.'

## A Corpse By the Road

The cultivation of perfect Wisdom and Compassion is the path of the Buddhas. But along the way it is easy to become attached to one, and neglect the other.

One day, the Seeker was approached by one of the senior monks, who said, 'Would you like to come with a few of us into the forest?'

'Yes,' replied the Seeker. 'Thank you, sir.'

So the visitor followed respectfully behind the senior monk and two of his young brothers as they left the monastery through the entrance gates. As they walked along a well-used path that took them deeper into the forest, it was not long before they passed by the corpse of a dog.

The Seeker stopped and looked at the body, spontaneously reciting some prayers and quietly wishing for an auspicious rebirth. But he noticed that none of the monks ahead of him had stopped and this made him curious.

When he eventually caught up with the group again, the Seeker directed his question to the senior monk in the lead, 'Excuse me, sir. The corpse we just passed by, I said a prayer for it. Did you?'

'It's dead,' was the senior monk's blunt reply.

'Yes, it is,' agreed the Seeker, 'but I was taught that Compassion is like a garden that needs to be cultivated, nurtured, in order to bear fruit later on.'

'No,' said the senior monk. 'Compassion comes out of Wisdom and the practice of detachment.'

'Thank you, sir,' replied the Seeker diplomatically, and they continued along the narrowed path.

## Banishment

One day, as the Seeker was walking around the grounds of the monastery, he passed by several small groups of young monks caught up in serious discussions. It was obvious that something unusual was happening and members of the Sangha, the monastic community, could be heard saying, 'It's not fair…everybody makes mistakes…the Abbot acts as if he's perfect.'

There was tension in the air and the Seeker wondered what was happening.

Later, after the last meal of the day, one of the old laymen he had helped a few days before came to his cabin, and said, 'You should know that the Assistant Abbot is leaving the monastery. Tomorrow morning he will be gone.'

'Did he do something wrong?' asked the Seeker.

'Yes,' replied the layman with a wry smile. 'He is popular with some of the Sangha.'

'Oh, but did he do anything wrong?'

'Not really, it's just about rumours and monastic politics.'

'Well, thank you for letting me know,' said the Seeker, bowing respectfully.

The old layman returned the bow and, before walking away, said, 'You can expect some of the other monks will eventually be leaving as well.'

Early the following morning, the Seeker watched as the Assistant Abbot walked out through the entrance gates for the last time. It was a sad scene.

Then the old layman he had been speaking with the day before came up to the Seeker, and said, 'See, over there, the Abbot is watching,' indicating an old monk standing by the gates with a look of satisfaction on his face.

The Seeker felt a deep sense of disillusionment. He went back to the cabin, packed up his small bag of belongings, and walked down the woodland path towards the garden.

## Pouring Nothing

Mind is the creator of worlds: of heavens and hells. The sighted can be held captive by it, as can the blind. Harmful habits of thought, speech and action are like the building blocks of a cell. Here the prisoner and the guard are one and the same.

Entering the garden once more, the Seeker immediately felt a sense of great peace. This place seemed to breathe wisdom and compassion. He looked around for the old teacher among the neat rows of fruit trees, but could not find him there. Neither was he to be seen working with the vegetables. Where was he? Just as the Seeker was beginning to wonder if the old man was still around, he noticed a small cabin in the distance. The young man walked over to it, tentatively knocked on the front door and waited. But no one came out and no sound could be heard from within.

The Seeker cautiously opened the door and peered inside. It was dark except for a large candle, the light from which allowed him to recognise the old Gardener seated on the floor with what looked like a rather large teapot and two cups in front of him.

The young man thought, 'Oh good, perhaps we can drink tea together and talk.' But as the Seeker approached, he noticed that the old man's eyes were closed. Was he meditating? The young man sat down facing him and decided there was nothing he could do except wait.

Unable to see daylight, it was impossible to know for sure the passage of time. The young man's aching knees eventually sent a message: that they might have been sitting for hours. He began to feel impatient. Why was the old man sitting by a teapot and two cups, yet was not using them? Surely any hot water in the teapot would be cold by now.

When the old man finally moved, it caught the Seeker by surprise. Slowly, still with his eyes closed, the old man lowered his right hand, picked up the teapot and, lifting it high over one of the cups, gracefully poured water into it without spilling a drop. How could he do that with his eyes closed, and know when to stop filling it? Then the old man gently placed the teapot back down on the floor and picked up the cup he had just filled. He lifted it high over the other cup and poured the contents into it, before pouring the water back into the teapot again. He performed this practice over and over, pouring from teapot to cup, cup to cup, and back again into the teapot. The Seeker looked on in wonder at the graceful beauty of this simple act.

Then, to the astonishment of the Seeker, the old man opened his eyes and gestured that he wanted his young student to take over. So with his right hand trembling nervously, he picked up the teapot and, with eyes closed, tried to copy the slow movements the Gardener had demonstrated. He started pouring water in the hope of finding one of the cups and, to his surprise, he heard the distinctive sound of a vessel being filled. The Seeker was very pleased with himself and placed the teapot back down on the floor. But before he had a chance to find the cup he had just filled, ice-cold water was poured over his head.

'Agh!' he exclaimed in shock, and opened his eyes in time to see the old man calmly placing the now empty cup back down on the floor.

The Seeker stared at the old man in stunned silence, unable to find any words except for an internal scream of 'Why?' But he sensed that this must be a lesson of some sort and decided to continue with the exercise. Once again, the young man blindly picked up the teapot and slowly lifted it over to where he thought the cups were. This time, to his disappointment, water splashed on the floor, and he placed the teapot back down. Again he felt the shock of ice-cold water being poured over his head.

'Agh!' he called out again, and opened his eyes in time to see the old man placing the teapot back down on the floor.

Feelings of frustration and resentment were building within the Seeker, but he was determined to succeed. So he closed his eyes and tried again and again, each time expecting to feel ice-cold water over his head. His whole body became soaked, and a strange numbness gradually enveloped him. The Seeker felt disorientated, but stubbornly carried on striving for perfection. This continued for some time, until eventually something within snapped and he realised his foolishness.

'Oh!' he exclaimed, opening his eyes. Then he peered into the teapot. It was empty. The Seeker looked at the old Gardener and together they burst out laughing like small children.

> Empty the vessel
> Filled to the brim
> Pour away Pride,
> Pour and begin.
>
> Set the child free
> For a moment to see
> Empty yet full,
> The world in a teapot.

## The Crying Woman

The Seeker was permitted to spend the night in the Gardener's small cabin, and felt at home. In the morning, he would ask if it would be possible to stay for a while. He secretly imagined remaining in the garden for the rest of his life with the old man as his teacher. Excited by the prospect of life in this refuge, at first he found it difficult to sleep. But eventually nature guided him towards rest.

In the hours just before sunrise, the Seeker had a dream in which he was transported to a place of snow-capped mountains and desolate valleys. He found himself at the base of an immense mountain, taller than any he had ever seen, and noticed long lines of people walking towards it, reaching their arms out as if trying to embrace a lover.

As the Seeker looked more closely, he saw that countless others had already arrived there and were desperately trying to climb to the summit high above the clouds. But there were so many people on the mountain that it was almost impossible to move. They jostled and fought. Many fell to their deaths and the base of the mountain was littered with corpses. Strangely, despite observing the shocking scene, the Seeker felt drawn to join the lines of people going towards the mountain, as if the urge to climb to the summit was the only purpose of life.

Then he heard the sound of a woman's voice wailing and crying in distress, like a mother who had lost her only child. The spell was broken, replaced instead with an intense feeling of concern for the woman's welfare. He looked around and was surprised to see her sitting nearby. He walked over to offer her comfort but, as he came closer, the sound of the woman's voice seemed to change and he realised that she was crying out to him. In that instant, the Seeker felt embraced by boundless compassion, and saw her as a Bodhisattva, trying to help suffering sentient beings like himself.

The Seeker woke up and smiled to himself, wondering why he was determined to climb mountains when he sensed that Home was so close. Maybe, he thought, the old Gardener could help him find the answer.

## The Light

The Seeker approached the old man to ask if he could stay with him in the garden. He had already imagined that the answer would be yes.

'This is a beautiful place and I feel at home here,' the young man began. 'You are an excellent teacher and I would like to be your student. Can I stay here with you?'

The old man smiled, took hold of the Seeker's hand and led him out of the garden into the woods. This was not what he had expected. Although confused, the young man obediently followed his teacher deeper into the forest. Suddenly, the old man stopped, pointed in the direction he wanted the Seeker to go, and left him alone in shock. Why had the old man done this? Was he sending him away? Not knowing what to think, the Seeker continued walking in the direction he had been shown.

Eventually, he came upon a small clearing in the forest and decided to rest in the shade of a large tree in the middle of it. A bell was hanging from one of its broad lower branches. The Seeker looked at the bell, wondering why it had been placed there. He noticed that there was no pole to strike it with, so he judged it to be just an old useless ornament. Soon he lost interest and sat down against the tree. It was not long before he fell asleep.

By the time he woke up, it was late in the day, so he thought it best to stay where he was. The young man sat in meditation for a while and an old teaching from the Buddha came to mind:

> Dwell! You are the Light itself. Rely on yourself. Do not rely on others. The Dharma is the light. Rely on the Dharma. Do not rely on anything other than the Dharma.

In that moment, the Seeker realised that ultimately there was no one who could help him except himself.

## The Demon's Face

Late in the night, the Seeker received a visitor to his forest.

'Good evening,' said the young man to the distant sound of breaking twigs.

Crack! replied the sound, now much closer than before.

Footsteps? thought the Seeker, sweat forming on his brow.

Beware now! was the thought that caused his heart to pound.
Then he saw the demon's face and smiled to himself.
Ah, welcome friend. Come sit with me. Come rest for a while.
But I might kill you! warned the demon, trying yet again.
Then you would die, the Seeker thought,
And fear disappeared.

The Buddha said,

> Hidden in the mystery of consciousness, the mind, incorporeal, flies alone far away. Those who set their mind in harmony become free from the bonds of death.
>
> Those who have a mind that is unsteady, who know not the path of Truth, whose faith and peace are ever wavering, they shall never reach fullness of wisdom.
>
> But those who have a mind that is calm and self-controlled are free from the lust of desires, who have risen above good and evil, they are awake and have no fear. (Dhammapada 37–39)

## The Funeral Procession

Early in the morning, while the Seeker was resting against a tree, nearby he noticed some movement amid the debris on the forest floor. Slight rustling sounds accompanied it, and then he saw a long line of ants marching like a victorious army through the clearing, carrying various trophies back to their nest. Everything on their backs was much larger and heavier than them, but with incredible strength and organisation they were managing to transport leaves, pieces of fruit, and insects.

Further back in the line, the Seeker was surprised to see a mass of heaving aggressive movement, as attacking ants were overwhelming something much larger. Whatever the poor creature was, it tried to lift its body in a desperate attempt to escape, but the ants intensified their onslaught, and soon it collapsed to the earth, dead.

The ants organised themselves and, working together, lifted up their latest kill. The Seeker saw that the body was a large frog. This was a jolt to the young man's perception of who he thought he was. Staring at the corpse as it passed by, the Seeker saw the facade of self stripped away, revealing the coarse and subtle remnants of his desires, fears, and opinions displayed clearly for him to learn from.

Deeply touched, the young man bowed to all the creatures and wished the frog an auspicious rebirth. Then he said, 'Thank you, little ones. You are, indeed, excellent teachers.'

## The Bell

Late in the afternoon, the Seeker felt thirsty and followed the sound of trickling water to a small stream in the forest. The water was sweet to taste and refreshingly cool so he decided to bathe himself. As he splashed water on to his face, the clear sound of a bell cut through this moment of pleasure. He wondered if he was imagining it and started to make his way back to the clearing to investigate.

The Seeker was surprised to find a little old woman sitting beneath the bell that hung from the large tree against which he had slept the night before. At first, he tried to imagine how she could have struck the bell, as it would have been too high for her to reach. He approached her respectfully and bowed. With palms joined together, she returned the bow, with the most infectious smile he had ever seen.

The old woman joyfully called out, '*Namo Amitabha! Namo Amitabha!*' laughing in between each phrase like a little girl.

'Good day, honoured Mother,' the Seeker said. 'How are you?'

'*Namo Amitabha. Namo Amitabha,*' was her reply.

Suddenly the Seeker heard the bell above them ring out by itself. The loud crisp sound broke through his hard ego. In that moment, something indescribable happened, changing his perspective. He looked around himself as if for the first time, like a small child. '*Namo Amitabha!*' the Seeker cried out with joy, feeling the embrace of boundless compassion.

Now young and old laughed together, free.

Later, the old woman calmly stood up and walked away into the forest, leaving the Seeker alone once more. But he wasn't concerned, picked up his small bag of belongings and continued on his way.

## A Sparrow Splashing

The Seeker continued walking through the forest until he reached its edge. He found himself in a fertile land of farms and gently rolling hills. A little further, he came upon a small village and stopped at a shop to buy a cool drink and some chocolate. The young man then walked over to a large tree, and sat down in its shade. He closed his eyes for a while and listened to the sound of splashing water coming from a nearby birdbath. When he opened his eyes again, an old man was standing over him.

'*Namo Amitabha*,' said the Seeker in greeting, with palms joined together in respect.

'What is *Amitabha*?' demanded the old man.

'A sparrow splashing in the birdbath,' replied the Seeker.

The old man paused for a moment, regarding the young stranger, and said, 'Before the Buddha left his mother's womb, he had already fulfilled his vow to save all sentient beings. Young man, tell me, what does that mean?'

'When the clouds have cleared, sunlight shines upon the water,' replied the Seeker.

'And where is your *Amitabha*-mind?' demanded the old man.

The Seeker held up his bag of pralines, and said, 'You are hungry; have a piece of chocolate.'

At that point the old man burst out laughing, and exclaimed, 'Ah, Buddhism lives!'

'More compost for the garden,' replied the Seeker.

The old man bowed to his young teacher and sat down, wishing to learn more from him.

Clouds dissolve
And yet there are tears.
Mountains are still mountains
Enjoy the view.

A playful child
The Teacher as student
As real as you
A sparrow splashing.

# The Teacher's Journey

## May I Be Happy

During a group retreat, a student was having difficulty following the Teacher's instruction to quietly say, 'May I be happy, may I be happy…'

When the bell was struck to end the meditation, the student was confused and angry. When the Teacher asked if any of the retreatants had questions, she took the opportunity to confront him, and said, 'What does this practice have to do with Buddhist selflessness?'

'Are you a Buddha?' asked the Teacher.

'No, of course not!' she exclaimed.

'Then what are you?' pressed the Teacher.

'Uh…human, I suppose,' she replied.

'OK,' said the Teacher, 'then work with that. There is a wall between you and others, like clouds that obscure the sun. "May I be happy, may all beings be happy" are ultimately the same. But until you can let go of like and dislike, good and bad, begin with "May I be happy." Also reflect on the universal wish for happiness. Then, one day, the light of your true happiness will disperse the clouds of ignorance and shine on all beings, excluding no one. So practise, practise. OK?'

'Yes, I will. Thank you for your teaching,' said the student, bowing.

## Born Again

In this world, there are different cultures, many ways to live. Along the way there will be misunderstanding, fear, frustration and anger. When the mirror of truth is held up to your face, what will it show you?

One day, a young woman on a mission came to see the Teacher, and said, 'Do you know the Lord?'

'Oh yes, for a long time,' replied the Teacher.

'But you are a Buddhist,' she said. 'You must repent of your sins, and be born again.'

'Born again. Oh yes, many times,' said the Teacher.

'What?' asked the woman in confusion.

'Caught in Samsaric suffering for countless lifetimes,' continued the Teacher.

Angrily, the woman exclaimed, 'You Buddhist, you will go to Hell!'

In response, the Teacher politely bowed, and said, 'Thank you for your teaching.'

The woman calmed down and left with a smile on her face. But what she did not know was that the Teacher had long prayed to be reborn in the Hell Realm and help alleviate the suffering of all sentient beings.

The Buddha said,

Victory brings hate, because the defeated are unhappy. Those who surrender victory and defeat find joy. (Dhammapada 201)

## Poisoned Arrows

One day, the Teacher came across two men debating each other about the existence of God. They were so carried away by their emotions, that they did not at first see him standing nearby.

'Look, there is no proof that God exists,' asserted one man.

'But you cannot prove that God does not exist,' replied the other much older man.

Eventually they noticed the Teacher, and turned to face him.

He greeted them with a bow, and the old man said, 'I am a Christian, and I think it's wonderful that you Buddhists believe in God.'

'Do we?' asked the Teacher.

'Buddhists are atheists, like me,' stated the young man. 'They don't believe in God.'

'Don't we?' questioned the Teacher.

The two men stopped talking and looked at the Teacher, confused.

'You speak of belief and non-belief in God,' began the Teacher. 'Well, the Buddha had a teaching related to this subject. Imagine that each of you has been struck by a poisoned arrow and right at this moment the poison is moving through your bodies. What will you do to save your lives?'

'Try to find an antidote,' said the old man.

'Yes, try to find an antidote,' agreed the other man.

'Good,' said the Teacher. 'The Buddha taught that a poisoned arrow symbolises the quest for God/no-god and other metaphysical questions. For those who practise the Buddha's teachings, the priority in this life is to fully understand the nature of our own suffering, by looking deeply into its causes and conditions, and so find the way out of suffering. To achieve this is like finding the antidote to poisoned arrows.'

'So you don't believe in God,' concluded the old Christian, disappointed.

The young man smiled and, noticing this, the Teacher said, 'A follower of the Buddha's way is not an atheist, nor an agnostic. If a label must be used, then it should be non-theistic. But if such names, labels, and opinions are habitually cherished, then they reinforce dualistic thinking, and further separate "I" from "You". This is where greed, anger, ignorance, jealousy and pride grow, causing much suffering for oneself and others. So the path to Buddhahood is the cultivation of perfect wisdom and compassion for the benefit of all sentient beings, excluding no one. Do you understand?'

Both men nodded.

## Heaven and Hell

A man who wandered the streets, tormented by the thoughts in his mind, came to the Teacher for advice. 'This place is hell,' the wanderer said. 'I want to leave. Where should I go?'

'Where is heaven?' asked the Teacher.

'I don't know,' replied the wanderer.

'Then how can you leave this place you call hell?'

'I don't know.'

The Teacher regarded the wanderer for a moment, and said, 'The Buddha taught that our life is the creation of our mind.'

'What do you mean?' asked the wanderer, looking frustrated.

'Mind is where You Are,' the Teacher stated. 'Hell is made of like and dislike. Leave it behind and the Pure Mind, home, is found. This is heaven.'

The wanderer bowed, and said, 'Thank you for your teaching.'

## A Flower is Growing

A man who wandered the streets, tormented by the thoughts in his mind, sought the Teacher for advice, and found him in a garden. 'I'm crazy,' the wanderer said, 'so tell me, what is real?'

'A flower is growing in the garden,' replied the Teacher.

'That is crazy!' exclaimed the wanderer, looking at the thousands of flowers blooming all around him.

'Samsara is Nirvana. Nirvana is Samsara,' said the Teacher.

'And more of nothing is less again,' replied the wanderer, frustrated.

The Teacher paused, regarding the wanderer. 'Look into the heart of form-emptiness, emptiness-form,' he advised.

The wanderer burst into tears. 'Please, tell me, what is real?' he pleaded.

The Teacher pointed at the wanderer, and said, 'A flower is growing in the garden.'

The wanderer stopped crying, and smiled. 'I am a flower!' he exclaimed.

'Good,' the Teacher encouraged. 'Getting closer.'

'Thank you,' said the wanderer, before he left, happily giggling to himself.

## A Wounded Tiger

One day, while the Teacher was walking through the streets of a town, he came upon a young man sitting in the gutter outside a pub, weeping. The Teacher said, 'Are you OK?'

'It's too late…it's too late,' sobbed the man drunkenly.

'What is?' asked the Teacher.

But the drunken man was not listening, and said, 'He killed us… killed us.'

Looking around, the Teacher could not see any bodies or trails of blood. 'Who hurt you and your friends?' he asked.

The drunken man stopped crying, and angrily exclaimed, 'The f—ing referee!'

Then the Teacher noticed the football club badge on the man's jacket, and understood. In that moment, all of the tens of thousands of suffering football fans in this world were represented by one wounded Tiger sobbing in the street.

## Unmasking Anger

'What about Anger?' asked a student.

'Who is angry?' questioned the Teacher.

'I am, sometimes,' replied the student.

'Who is this *I* you speak of?' asked the Teacher. 'Where is *I*? Find it for me.'

The student tried to follow the instructions, but became quite frustrated. 'I can't find it,' declared the student.

'Then what is Anger?' pressed the Teacher. 'What is its source?'

The student thought for a moment, and said, 'Well, I feel frustrated sometimes.'

'Dig deeper,' advised the Teacher. 'What is its source?'

'What do you mean?' asked the student, confused.

The Teacher regarded the student for a moment, and said, 'Are there times of joy and great happiness in your life?'

'Yes, of course!' replied the student. 'Everyone desires happiness.'

'Then how do you feel when those emotions end?' asked the Teacher.

'Frustrated… Oh!' exclaimed the student, gaining some insight.

'Keep on looking,' suggested the Teacher. 'Keep on stripping away. There is much more.'

## Weapons of Mass Destruction

One day, the Teacher witnessed a double murder. At a bus stop, a man and a woman were shouting at each other.

'You never listen to me!' screamed the woman.

'You lied to me, again!' roared the man.

'I'll f—ing kill you!' shrieked the woman.

'You're dead!' exclaimed the man, and raised his fist to strike the woman.

But at that point, they both stopped in their tracks, stunned. Why? A Buddhist Monk, the Teacher, was facing them. With the palms of his hands joined together, he bowed to the two of them, and calmly walked away.

The destructive forces that come from attachment, anger, and ignorance affect lives in unimaginable ways.

The Buddha said,

> What we are today comes from our thoughts of yesterday, and our present thoughts build our life of tomorrow: our life is the creation of our mind. If a person speaks or acts with an impure mind, suffering follows them as the wheel of the cart follows the beast that draws the cart.
>
> What we are today comes from our thoughts of yesterday, and our present thoughts build our life of tomorrow: our life is the creation of our mind. If a person speaks or acts with a pure mind, joy follows them as their own shadow.
>
> 'They insulted me, they hurt me, they defeated me, they robbed me.' Those who think such thoughts will not be free from hate.

For hate is not conquered by hate: hate is conquered by love. This is an eternal law.

Many do not know that we are here in this world to live in harmony. Those who know this do not fight against each other. (Dhammapada 1–6)

## Buttons

While on a silent group retreat, a student asked for a private interview with the Teacher. When the student entered the room where the Teacher was, he bowed respectfully, sat down facing him, and said, 'There is a problem with the cook. He keeps pushing my buttons.'

'Pushing whose buttons?' asked the Teacher.

'My buttons,' replied the student, slightly confused.

'Oh,' said the Teacher, 'and who created those buttons?'

'What?' asked the student. 'I don't understand. You see, there is a problem…'

'Yes,' interrupted the Teacher, 'there is a problem. Tell me, who created it?'

'Well,' said the student, 'as I was trying to say, the cook refuses to make eye contact with me at meal times each day.'

The Teacher regarded the student for a moment, and said, 'You do know that this is a silent retreat, and that all students should refrain from making eye contact with each other?'

'Yes, I know,' replied the student. 'But surely the cook is exempt. You see, back home I'm used to a certain standard of service from staff…'

The Teacher loudly clapped his hands, interrupting, and said, 'You are not home now, and neither is the cook. You are here with me, and he is not. So tell me, whose thoughts created this problem?'

The student paused to reflect, then said, 'I have created this problem. I'm sorry, I didn't understand.'

'And who created those buttons?' pressed the Teacher.

'I did,' replied the student, now understanding.

## The Most Difficult Person

While on a group retreat, a student asked for a private interview with the Teacher. He entered the room where the Teacher was, bowed respectfully, and sat down facing him. 'I have a problem with angry thoughts,' the student began. 'But I'm not sure you will understand.'

'Oh, why not?' asked the Teacher.

'Because you don't get angry,' declared the student.

'Don't I?' queried the Teacher.

'Well,' said the student, 'you are so calm and patient with people. I doubt that you would have an enemy in this world.'

The Teacher regarded the student for a moment, then said, 'You say I have no enemies. That is correct – I have no enemies. But I know a very difficult person who used to drive me crazy with constant chatter and would never leave me alone.'

'That sounds terrible!' exclaimed the student. 'What did you do?'

'First I invited them in, and then let them go,' replied the Teacher.

'What? I don't understand,' questioned the student. 'Why would you invite them in if you wanted to be left alone? And what does "let them go" mean?'

'Thoughts,' said the Teacher. 'Harmful thoughts cannot be forced to go away, and fighting them only increases their power. So relax, invite them in, and soon the brain-mind will get bored and let them go away naturally, as all created things eventually do. Also, understand that the most difficult person you will ever meet is yourself.'

The student smiled, and said, 'Thank you for your teaching,' bowing respectfully before leaving.

## A Compassionate Heart

One day, the Teacher was asked to help a Buddhist patient in hospital and a visiting monk from another lineage accompanied him. While walking through the main corridor, they came across a woman who seemed upset about something. To the irritation of his companion, the Teacher stopped to speak with her.

'Excuse me,' said the Teacher. 'Are you all right?'

The woman turned to face the Teacher and, with her body trembling, said, 'No, I'm not…' before she burst into tears and her arms reached out hesitantly towards him.

He noticed what she was doing, and asked, 'Do you need a hug?'

'Oh yes,' she responded, before falling into the Teacher's arms, sobbing.

The visiting monk looked on with surprise and disgust written on his face.

Eventually, the woman regained her composure and let go of the Teacher. 'Thank you,' she said. 'You Buddhists are good and kind people.'

'Can I help you in any way?' asked the Teacher.

'No, bless you. You've done more than enough already,' she replied. 'My husband is dying and my sons are with him. I'm the one who has to be strong for the family.'

She looked at the Teacher one last time, wiped the remaining tears from her eyes, and went back into the room where her dying husband and sons were.

The Teacher continued on his way with the monk, who now seemed visibly troubled by something.

'Are you all right?' asked the Teacher.

'You shouldn't have done that,' said the monk.

'What are you talking about?' pressed the Teacher, knowing full well what was bothering his fundamentalist companion.

'You should not have held that woman,' asserted the monk.

'I left that woman back with her family,' replied the Teacher. 'It is you who are holding on to her.'

## Hell College

A young woman, with an elderly friend, attended a class at the Teacher's temple. When the two women looked at the Buddha altar, they were upset by what they found and determined to speak to the

Teacher about it. An opportunity presented itself later during a talk he was giving about the Buddhist Hell Realm.

'Do any of you have questions?' asked the Teacher, looking around at his students.

'Yes, I do,' responded the young woman. 'You were just speaking about Buddhist Hell. I am Jewish. My grandparents lived through the hell that the Nazis created in Europe and many of our family were exterminated in the concentration camps. I want to know why there are swastikas on those three Buddha statues on your altar?'

The Teacher regarded the woman for a moment, and said, 'I am sorry for the suffering that your family and countless others experienced at the hands of the Nazis. Their twisted ideology and actions were the embodiment of hatred, greed, ignorance, jealousy and pride. But, if you look closely at the symbols on those Buddhas, you will notice that they are the reverse of what you might be familiar with. See, the Nazis couldn't even get that right…'

Most of the students laughed, but not the young woman, or her friend.

The Teacher continued. 'What you call the swastika is, in fact, an ancient sacred symbol for many diverse spiritual traditions around this world: in Asia, the Middle East, and even Europe thousands of years ago. Today it is often seen on Buddhist and Hindu architecture, sacred texts, mandalas and other objects like the statues on our altar here.'

Then the Teacher paused, and said, 'When I look at this symbol on sacred objects, I am reminded of an ancient connection with the Buddha and all sentient beings in this world through the ages. The Nazis lost the war, and their perverse ideology will continue to lose if we practise love, not hatred and bigotry.'

'I agree,' replied the young woman, 'but I need time to reflect on my feelings about this. Thank you.'

Then her elderly friend spoke up. 'But what about Hitler? Is he still suffering in your Buddhist Hell?'

'Hitler is no doubt suffering in a hell of his own creation. But even though it may seem to him like eternal damnation, it is not. Eventually he, like all sentient beings, will attain Buddhahood.'

The old woman looked horrified by what she had just heard, and said, 'I am a Christian and believe that God would forgive Hitler only if he repented of his evil.'

The Teacher regarded the woman for a moment, and said, 'From a Buddhist perspective, Hitler, Francis of Assisi, Stalin, Gandhi…all have the same essential nature. But Karma, their accumulated thoughts, speech and actions are different. So they, like us, create heavens or hells for themselves in the present and future. For Buddhists, there is no divine punishment. There is enough self-inflicted suffering in this and future lives to take care of that.'

The irony of this statement was acknowledged by laughter from the students.

Then the Teacher looked at the old woman, and said, 'For Buddhists, the Hell Realm is like a training college. Eventually everyone graduates, but for some, like Hitler, it may take aeons. Understand?'

'I understand,' replied the old woman. 'Thank you.'

## Tasting Coffee

A group of students arranged to meet with the Teacher in a café, which had been privately booked for the occasion. What they did not know was that the Teacher had asked the barista to hide in the kitchen. When the students saw their Teacher behind the coffee machine, they were surprised. Eventually they started giving the Teacher their orders. All was going well, until a few people began to loudly debate each other.

'A cup and the coffee in it are the same,' asserted a young man.

'No, they're different,' responded a woman.

Another man intervened. 'You're both wrong. It's neither.' Pleased with his apparent victory, he got up from his table and walked over to a nearby counter where the Teacher was, and said, 'Can I have a cup of coffee, please?'

The Teacher presented the man with an empty cup.

'What's this?' asked the student.

'You know,' replied the Teacher.

'Well, it's not coffee,' said the student, who then watched in stunned silence as the Teacher began pouring the contents of a pot of coffee on to the counter and let it dribble to the floor below.

'What is this?' asked the Teacher.

'Please, just fill my cup!' pleaded the man.

The Teacher took the cup back from the man and threw it to the floor, breaking it into many pieces. 'It is full,' said the Teacher. 'Taste it.'

As the student stared at the pieces of the shattered cup lying in pools of spilled coffee, he started to laugh. It was the best thing he had ever tasted.

> Dualistic views
> Of right and wrong are easily shattered,
> Mind scattered and lost.
>
> Just drink in the essence,
> Live in the Way;
> Free of contrivance
> No boundaries are seen.

## One Path, Many Ways

One day, a young man came to visit the Teacher at his home, bowed respectfully, and said, 'I am unhappy and feel that I should ordain as a monk. What do you think?'

'As a monk you could also be unhappy,' the Teacher pointed out.

'But I dream of becoming a monk,' insisted the young man.

The Teacher regarded him for a moment, and said, 'Are you married?'

'Yes,' he replied.

'And do you have any children?'

'Yes, I have two children, a son and a daughter.'

'Then that is the life you have created for yourself and others. Your wife and children still have much to teach you.'

'They teach me? What do you mean?'

'There are many ways to train as a Bodhisattva,' said the Teacher. 'Monk, priest, yogi, householder, just to name a few. They are all valid paths and no one way is superior to the others. You not only have a responsibility to care for your family, but your life presents countless opportunities to learn and practise.'

'But how?' asked the young man.

'When your children look at you, what do you see in their eyes?' prompted the Teacher.

'Love... Oh!' exclaimed the young man, beginning to understand.

'And from your wife?' asked the Teacher.

'The same, except when I disappoint her, and then she teaches me a lesson,' laughed the young man.

'Why do you think she is disappointed with you sometimes?'

'Because I don't spend as much time with her and the children as she would like.'

'And do you think she's right?'

'Yes, but I need to be alone to practise meditation.'

'Does your wife meditate?' asked the Teacher.

'Yes, but someone has to take care of the children.'

'Then take it in turns, or practise with your family.'

'With the children? But my daughter's only six and my son is just five years old!'

'I began at five years of age,' said the Teacher. 'You are their father. Teach them. It will be good for the children in many ways, and you will have the opportunity to cultivate virtue, wisdom and compassion. Don't forget that there is much more to the practice than just meditation. Your family is a precious resource, if only you give them a chance. Now go to them, and remember that the path of a householder is a noble one, which has eventually led many sentient beings to Buddhahood.'

Tears of gratitude rolled down the young man's cheeks. He bowed, and said, 'Thank you for your teaching.'

## I Bow to You

One day, a little boy saw the Teacher bowing to a Buddha altar and wondered what he was doing. The boy got to his feet, walked over to the Teacher, and said, 'Who are you bowing to?'

'To you,' replied the Teacher.

'To me?' questioned the surprised little boy.

The Teacher regarded the boy for a moment, and said, 'I bow to the earth, the sky, the oceans, rocks, trees, all beings, all Buddha. Yes, I bow to you.'

The little boy smiled, put the palms of his hands together and bowed to his Teacher.

The child and Master are one
In mind and heart,
And the Seeker knows this
If nothing else.

A life within a dream
Real as clouds,
But on awakening
Self and other vanish.

Pursuing fame and fortune,
Kingdoms of desire won't suffice;
Just rest in the essence of mind
And all Is.

Old habits of mind dissolve,
Thoughts quiet of themselves;
Free of notions of self and no-self
All is dharmata.

The moment this is realised
The Teacher is seen
As mind clear and open,
A sparrow splashing in the birdbath.

# Glossary

Amitabha: the Buddha of Infinite Light. A transhistorical Buddha venerated by many Buddhist lineages and schools, like Ch'an, Zen, Vajrayana, Tien T'ai, and particularly Pure Land. Amitabha Buddha at the highest level of understanding represents the True Mind, the self-nature common to the Buddhas and sentient beings – all-encompassing and all-inclusive.

Avalokiteshvara: Bodhisattva of Compassion. Disciple of Amitabha Buddha. Also called Kuan-Yin in Chinese Buddhist schools like Ch'an and Pure Land.

Bodhisattva: Enlightened Being or Heroic Mind. One who has vowed to attain complete enlightenment for him or herself and all sentient beings, and is committed to the cultivation of perfect compassion and wisdom.

Buddha: Awakened One. An individual who has attained complete enlightenment, such as the historical Buddha Shakyamuni who lived over 2,500 years ago.

Buddhahood: the realisation of complete enlightenment. Rather than something to attain, it is the natural and continuous experience of our essence.

Buddha-nature: the essential nature of all sentient beings. The inner potential for complete enlightenment.

Ch'an: a major school of Chinese Buddhism, with several branches. In other Asian languages, Ch'an is translated as Zen, Seon and Thien.

Dana: Generosity. An important Buddhist practice earning merit, good Karma.

Dharma: 1. any recognised truth, such as 'the sky is blue'; 2. the teachings of the Buddha: Buddha-Dharma.

Dharmata: Suchness. Things as they truly are, without any distortion or obscuration.

Dukkha: the Dissatisfied Mind, or the Unsatisfactoriness of Life. Often translated as 'suffering'. Dukkha is a central teaching of the Buddha.

Emptiness: A central theme in Buddhism, indicating the lack of any truly existing independent nature of any and all phenomena. Positively stated, phenomena do exist but as mere appearances, interdependent manifestations of mind with no limitations. It is not just the mind of an individual, as mind is also free of any ultimately true existence.

Hell Realm: one of the Six Realms of Samsara. Characterised by intense habitual feelings of aggression. The other five are the god realm of pride; jealous gods; human realm; animal realm; and hungry ghosts.

Karma: Action. The unerring law of cause and effect; that is, positive actions bring happiness, and negative actions bring suffering in this or some future life.

Mantra: a particular combination of sounds symbolising the nature of a deity. These sacred invocations are recited in different languages, such as Sanskrit, and the syllables in their structure represent various energies which flow through the practice.

Merit: good Karma earned through virtuous deeds and thoughts. There is also the ancient practice of merit transference, or sharing one's own merit and virtue with all beings. At the end of many Buddhist services is this prayer: 'We dedicate the merit gained from this practice to the complete enlightenment of all sentient beings.' This practice is part of the cultivation of selflessness.

Namo Amida Butsu: 'I entrust myself to the Buddha of Boundless Light and Life.' A Japanese transliteration of the Sanskrit 'Namo Amitabha Buddha.'

Namo Amitabha: a mantra used in oral recitation practice by followers of Pure Land Buddhism, often abbreviated to just Amitabha.

Nirvana: Extinguished. Complete extinction of individual existence; cessation of rebirth and entry into bliss. Liberation from samsaric suffering.

Om Mani Padme Hum: the Mantra of Compassion in Himalayan Buddhist lineages. It is believed to embody the compassion and blessings of Avalokiteshvara Bodhisattva.

Samsara: Cyclic Existence. Realms of birth and death. An endless cycle of rebirth and suffering.

Sangha: one of the Three Jewels, the other two being the Buddha and the Dharma. It refers to the followers of Buddhism, particularly the community of ordained monks and nuns.

Sending and Taking: a powerful Buddhist practice of cultivating compassion for the suffering of others. It is widely taught in Himalayan Buddhist schools, which call it Tonglen but originally it was brought to Tibet by an Indian monk, Atisha Dipankara, who had studied for years on the island of Sumatra, in modern-day Indonesia.

Sutra: a sacred text describing sermons given by the Buddha. There are many sutras.

Ten Directions: the four cardinal and inter-cardinal points of a compass, and up and down.

Yogi: a Tantric Buddhist practitioner.

www.ingramcontent.com/pod-product-compliance
Lightning Source LLC
Chambersburg PA
CBHW062156100526
44589CB00014B/1856